I0555296

My Amazing Toddler
Behavioral Series

I Put My Toys Away.

I Clean UP!

An Affirmation-Themed Toddler Book
About Cleaning Up (Ages 2-4)

By Suzanne T. Christian

TWO RAVENS
B O O K S

Two Little Ravens
CHILDREN'S NON-FICTION BOOKS

Copyright © 2025 by Two Little Ravens,
an imprint of Two Ravens Books LLC.

All rights reserved.

No part of this book may be reproduced or used in any way or form or by any means whether electronic or mechanical. This means that you cannot record or photocopy any material ideas or tips that are provided in this book, without the prior written permission of the copyright owner.

Paperback Edition: 9781968080341
Hardcover Edition: 9781968080358
Digital Edition: 9781968080365

Published in the United States by Two Ravens Books LLC,
254 Chapman Rd, Ste 209, Newark DE 19702

'Expand the mind, free the imagination, one title at a time.'
www.tworavensbooks.com

Welcome to
"I Put My Toys Away. I Clean Up!"

This book is a playful collection of simple affirmations created just for toddlers. As you read together, your child will discover that cleanup time can be fun, rewarding, and something to look forward to.

Each page offers cheerful phrases and relatable routines that make tidying up feel like a game. With affirmations such as "Hooray! I Clean Up!" your child will build confidence, independence, and a sense of teamwork.

Remember, this book is not a quick fix. True change happens through repetition. By making it part of your daily reading routine, your toddler will gradually learn and embrace healthy cleanup habits that last.

Get ready for a journey of confidence, cooperation, and joyful cleanup moments with your little one!

Suzanne T. Christian

Clean-up time is
fun time!
I love to sing my
clean-up song.

I can do it all
by myself.
I Clean up!

I put my toys away.
I Clean Up!

Blocks go
"clack clack"
in the box.

My teddy says,
"Thank you!"
when I tuck him in.

Books like to sit together on the shelf.

Shoes go on the stand.
I Clean Up!

Crayons sleep in their box.
"Nighty-night!"

I make my room happy when it's tidy.

I hop like a bunny while picking up my toys.

I count many toys in the basket.

I'm a little helper when I tidy up!

I do my little wiggle
dance while I clean up.

I clean up with my family.
Teamwork!

I find lost toys when
I clean up. Surprise!

I clean up before
snack time.
I'm a big kid!

I clean up
before bedtime.
Goodnight, toys.

I clap, I cheer, when I am done. **Hooray!**

I Put My Toys Away.

I Clean UP!

The End!

My Amazing Toddler Behavioral Series

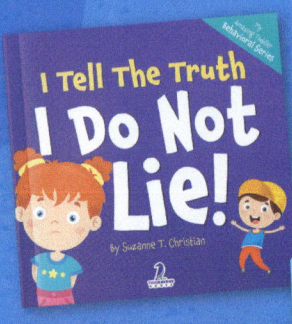

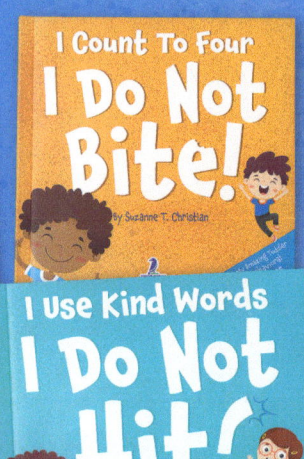

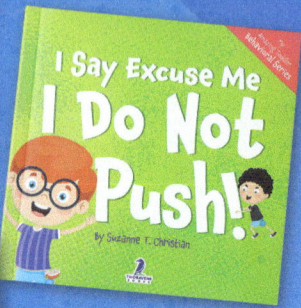

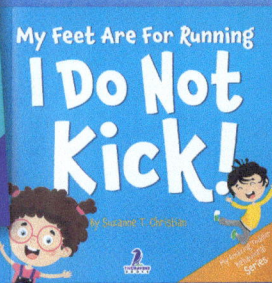

Check Out
Suzanne T. Christian's beloved series
'My Amazing Toddler Behavioral Series'.
Young readers are sure to enjoy!

Two Little Ravens
CHILDREN'S NON-FICTION BOOKS

Dear Amazing Reader,

Thank you for diving into **I Put My Toys Away. I Clean Up!** with me. If this book touched your heart or made a difference for a young reader, I'd be grateful if you could share your thoughts in a review. Your feedback inspires my future work and helps others discover the magic within these pages.

I'd love to hear from you directly if you have suggestions or ideas for improving the book. Please feel free to reach out to me at **suzanne.christian@tworavensbooks.com.** Your voice counts, and I cherish it deeply.

With heartfelt gratitude,

www.ingramcontent.com/pod-product-compliance
Lightning Source LLC
Chambersburg PA
CBHW041444120626
46547CB00002B/348